I'm Not Scared!

JER

ILLUSTRATED BY: ASHLYNN SIMPSON

Print information available on the last page

Rev. date: 04/03/2019

To order additional copies of this book, contact:
Xlibris
1-888-795-4274
www.Xlibris.com
Orders@Xlibris.com

On a hot beaming day as the sun arose Lizzie made a mad dash to the boat.

The boat was white, with a blue stripe, as big as a car and had an engine on the back with a canopy on top.

"Good Morning, my name is Mr. Ron and I will be the Captain for the day and to my left is Master Diver Mark."

"What are we doing today Captain Ron?", Lizzie asked.

"Well, today we're going snorkeling under the sea." he replied.

"Under the sea, but I'm scared..." she says with such excitement and fright.

"Why are you scared of the sea? It's beautiful and we should learn to protect it." Capt. Ron says.

"I do love the sea and the fish in it Capt. Ron." Lizzie replies.

"Lizzie, come with me and you won't be afraid anymore." Capt. Ron said softly.

"Life that lives in the sea is to be respected and protected. As long as you respect them, they will respect you." he said,

"Let's get on the boat and check it out!"

"We'll begin with a safety talk, the do's and don'ts. First, spray your goggles with this, it helps. Second, dump the extra out and put your fins on your feet. Lastly, when you're on the side of the boat when you're ready to go."

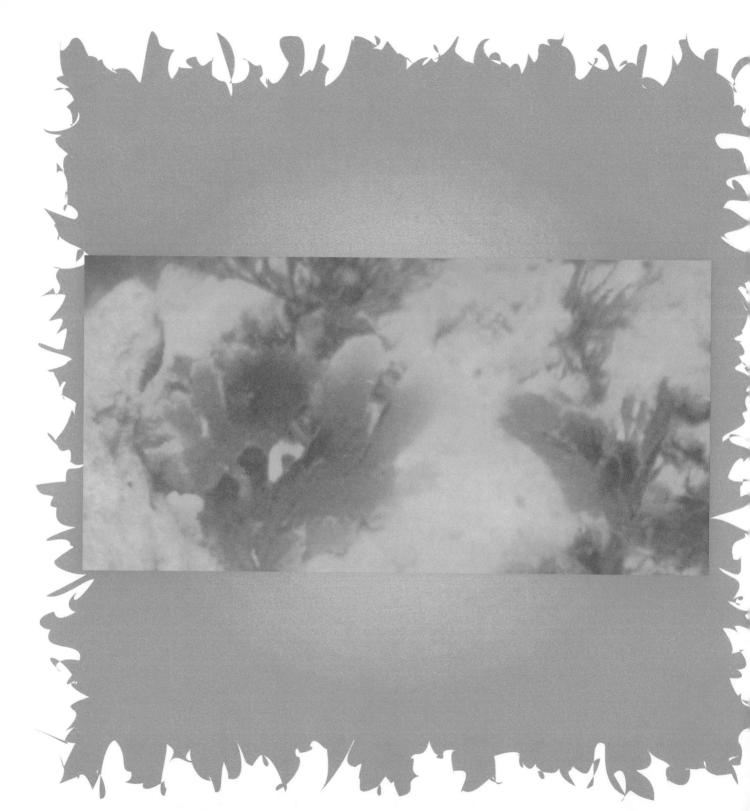

"While you're in the water do not touch anything because, the animals will get scared. You will see many different colors of fish just like you see many different types of people. You will see all different shapes of fish."

"Don't be afraid. Captain Ron is here! Is everyone one Ready? Set, Go!!"

When her time was up, her friends were giving her hugs and singing with joy. She was not afraid anymore.

When Liz returned home, she told her parents she was no longer afraid of swimming in the water where her feet couldn't touch the bottom.

Thank you, Captain Ron.

Boat

Car

Fish

Feet

Goggles

House

Sea

Swimming

Unscramble Words

_____   abot

_____   rca

_____   sfhi

_____   etfe

_____   glegsog

_____   sohue

_____   ase

_____   mgwnismi

This book is dedicated to Captain Ron who helped me over-come my fear of my feet not being able to touch the bottom of the ocean floor. When I was a young child I grew up around the water but due to an adult not paying attention an incident happened which changed my outlook on water. One trip with Capt. Ron treating me like family changed my outlook and now "I'm Not Scared" anymore. Thank you so much for helping me overcome something that affected my life and I will be seeing you again my friend. Maybe our next conversation can be about "Love Having No Boundaries"?

Printed in the United States
By Bookmasters